T0298800

# Informal Entrepreneurship and Cross-Border Trade in Maputo, Mozambique

Inês Raimundo and Abel Chikanda

**SAMP MIGRATION POLICY SERIES NO. 73**

**Series Editor: Prof. Jonathan Crush**

Southern African Migration Programme (SAMP)
2016

AUTHORS

Inês Raimundo is Associate Professor, Faculty of Arts and Social Sciences, Eduardo Mondlane University, Maputo, Mozambique.

Abel Chikanda is Assistant Professor of Geography and African & African American Studies, University of Kansas, Lawrence, Kansas, United States.

ACKNOWLEDGEMENTS

SAMP and its partners acknowledge the support of the IDRC for funding the Growing Informal Cities Project and this publication. The editor and the authors would like to thank the following for their assistance with the Maputo research and this report: Ramos Muanamoha (EMU), Paul Okwi (IDRC), Edgard Rodriguez (IDRC) and Bronwen Dachs.

Published by the Southern African Migration Programme, International Migration Research Centre, Balsillie School of International Affairs, Waterloo, Ontario, Canada

First published 2016

ISBN 978-1-920596-20-0

Cover photo: Xipamanine market in Maputo, Mozambique. By Rosino (Flickr) [CC BY-SA 2.0 (http://creativecommons.org/licenses/by-sa/2.0)], via Wikimedia Commons

Production by Bronwen Dachs Muller, Cape Town

Printed by Megadigital, Cape Town

# CONTENTS

# LIST OF TABLES

## LIST OF FIGURES

# EXECUTIVE SUMMARY

Nearly two-thirds (65%) of the economically-active population in Maputo is involved in one way or another in the informal sector. Many people operate outside of the recognized formal market system and frequently find themselves at odds with law enforcement agents. The expressions *dumba nengue* (trust your feet) and *dumba kutsutsuma* (run if you can) are used to refer to activities in the informal economy and clearly reflect the tensions between informal traders and law enforcement agents. Compared with other cities in the region, however, Maputo has traditionally adopted a more tolerant approach to the informal economy.

Informal cross-border trading is an essential part of Maputo's informal economy. The sheer numbers of traders at the country's major border crossings (especially at Lebombo with South Africa) is evidence of their contribution to the local as well as regional economy. This report presents the results of a SAMP survey of informal entrepreneurs connected to cross-border trade between Johannesburg and Maputo in 2014. The study sought to enhance the evidence base on the links between migration and informal entrepreneurship in Southern African cities and to examine the implications for municipal, national and regional policy. The GIC questionnaire was administered to a sample of 403 informal traders in seven markets in Maputo. The sample was divided into three entrepreneurial categories, namely traders who travel to and from Johannesburg to buy goods in South Africa and sell them in Maputo (61% of the sample); traders who travel to and from Johannesburg to buy goods in South Africa and sell them to other informal traders in Maputo (14%); and informal traders who do not travel, but buy goods from cross-border traders for resale (29%).

There were more men than women (56% to 44%) in the sample, largely because many women cross borders to buy goods while the selling of the products back home is done by their partners or sons. The predominance of women in cross-border trading has been attributed to various factors including their long history of crossing borders dating back to the early days of Mozambican independence and their experience in dealing with customs officials and wholesale storehouse managers in Johannesburg and other South African cities.

The entrepreneurial orientation of the traders was measured on a 28-factor scale, ranging from 1 (no importance) to 5 (extremely important). These factors were grouped into four types: financial benefits/security; market/business opportunities; intrinsic/personal rewards; and building human/social capital. As a group, financial benefits/security motivations were the most important factors and building human/social capital motivations the least. The most important financial factors (and the most important factors overall) included the need to give the family greater financial security and the need for more money just to survive. However, market/business related factors scored almost as high as the main survivalist factors. Here, wanting to run their own business, expanding an existing business and having a good idea for a product to sell in Mozambique all rated highly. Intrinsic/personal rewards were less important than economic factors. Finally, factors relating to building human/social capital were generally unimportant, with the exception of a general desire to contribute to the development of Mozambique.

The study sought to establish whether the informal entrepreneurs had been "pushed" into the informal sector by unemployment. Only 26% of the respondents were unemployed before they started their business, and another 19% had been students. The rest were employed before they started the informal business. The overwhelming majority of the respondents started their businesses from a very low capital base; mostly from personal savings. Access to formal sources of business capital was limited, which is a general reflection of the lack of support given to informal enterprises by formal financial institutions.

The main objective of the study was to examine the linkages and flows between Maputo and Johannesburg. The following findings were of significance:

- On average, the cross-border traders spend 1.52 days in South Africa on each trip. As many as 54% travel to Johannesburg at least once a week, which translates into nearly 80 days per year spent in South Africa. A further 34% travel there at least once a month, which translates into 18 days per year in South Africa.

- All of the traders purchased goods in Johannesburg but more than a third also bought goods in other places in South Africa, particularly in towns close to the Mozambican border such as Nelspruit, Malelane and Komatipoort. A few entrepreneurs (around 12%) also travel to neighbouring countries such as Swaziland, as well as to China, Dubai and other countries further afield to conduct business.

- Most of the traders sell the goods from South Africa in Maputo, Mozambique's capital, while a small number (less than 5%) also sell in other cities such as Xai Xai and Beira. The goods are sold mainly in their own shops in the informal sector (38%) or in their own stall in an informal market (24%). However, there is also evidence of informal-formal sector linkages with 9% selling in their own shop in the formal sector, 8% selling to retailers, 3% to wholesalers and 1% to restaurant owners.

- In terms of job creation, these business owners employed a total of 424 people. Half (51%) generated employment, with an average of 2.1 jobs per business. A significant proportion of the traders employ more than one person: 27% of those providing employment had two employees, 10% had three employees and 5% had four or more.

- Participation in trader organizations was generally low. The greatest level of participation amongst the traders was in *xitique* (money/savings clubs) (at 41%) where they can access business finance at concessionary rates. Participation in organized traders' associations was even lower, with only 6% of the traders indicating membership.

- A key question was whether cross-border traders generate incomes comparable to those of employees in the formal sector. The traders generated an average of ZAR22,000 per month in total sales and a profit of ZAR7,100 per month.

- The profits generated from informal businesses play an important role in meeting personal (79%) and family (77%) needs. A quarter of respondents were investing the proceeds in the education of family members, more than the proportion re-investing income in the business itself (only 19%). A third said that profits were being saved.

The study also documented some of the important contributions cross-border traders make to the South African economy:

- Informal trade contributes to South Africa's massive trade surplus with Mozambique.

- A wide variety of outlets in South Africa benefit from patronage by Mozambican traders, including wholesalers, supermarkets, small retailers (formal and informal), factories, farms and fresh produce markets. Easily the most important beneficiaries of Mozambican patronage are South African wholesalers (used by 48%).

- Another beneficiary is the South African Treasury. Most of the prices paid by traders for their goods include VAT. On their most recent trip to South Africa, however, only 55% had claimed the VAT refunds to which they were entitled. Of those who did not claim VAT, nearly half said they did not know the procedure and 36% said that the refund process took too long.

- Traders spend money on transportation, accommodation and food when in South Africa. About 37% usually pay for accommodation in rented rooms, hotels, guesthouses and B&Bs. The most common way for traders to travel to and from Johannesburg is on public transport, including buses (used by 43%), trucks (15%), and taxis (11%).

- The cross-border traders reported spending an average of ZAR14,300 on goods, ZAR1,700 on customs duties, ZAR1,441 on transportation, ZAR218 on accommodation and ZAR258 on other expenses on their most recent trip to South Africa. In total, a trader travelling from Maputo to Johannesburg spends approximately ZAR17,900 per trip on business-related costs.

In general, traders do not have problems with their documentation and immigration status when in South Africa. The introduction of a visa exemption for Mozambicans certainly played a significant role low in reducing undocumented migration. Three-quarters of the respondents (74%) hold visitors' permits when they travel to South Africa. The most important border or customs-related problem cited by the cross-border traders was corruption, experienced often or sometimes by 86% of the respondents. Others claimed that the duties they pay at the border are too high (85%), while long queues, congestion and delays at the border are often experienced by 82% of the cross-border traders. Some use intermediaries who know how to deal with customs officials to avoid paying the high duties.

The other challenges faced by the traders in their daily operations can be divided into two categories: those experienced while conducting business operations in Mozambique and those encountered when travelling to South Africa for business. In Mozambique, the most common problems related to competition from other traders, competition from large retailers or supermarkets, problems securing a selling site, conflicts with other traders and confiscation of merchandise. Theft of goods was cited as a common problem experienced by the traders on their way home from South Africa. In South Africa, the biggest challenges related to the difficulties of finding an affordable and safe place to stay in Johannesburg, prejudice against their nationality, harassment by the police or municipal authorities, and harassment by South African traders.

Cross-border trading has become a way of life for many in Mozambique, geographically encompassing every part of the country. From a gender perspective, women are more involved in cross-border trading activities and men are mainly involved in the sale of the products brought back from South Africa. The traders are clearly playing a key role in supplying commodities that are in scarce supply. Even though the sector occupies an important segment of the Mozambican economy, the traders receive little support from local and municipal authorities and the private sector. Access to finance remains a major hindrance to the success of the businesses as neither the government nor private banks provide loans to the traders.

Given the importance of informal cross-border trade, there is a need to include the informal traders in the country's poverty alleviation strategy. Even though they are regarded as informal, they pay fees to the local authorities for access to trading sites. They also buy goods in South Africa, some of which are sold to formal retailers, thereby blurring the formal-informal boundary. The informal tag therefore becomes a hindrance when considering the functioning of the Mozambican economy. The traders need to be seen as an essential component of the economy because, in their absence, Mozambique would be very different and poorer than it is today.

# INTRODUCTION

Although Mozambique has posted impressive macro-economic growth rates in recent years, there has been limited formal employment generation.[1] Most of the country's urban working population are thus still in the so-called informal economy.[2] The 2010 Maputo Structure Plan notes that nearly two-thirds (65%) of the economically active population in Maputo City is involved in some way in the informal sector.[3] The major activities include commerce and transport (50%), industry and construction (14%), agriculture (11%) and services (26%). A 2007 survey in Maputo found that 70% of households were involved in informal economic activities, with a significantly higher participation rate by female-headed households (86%) than male-headed households (62%).[4] The 2008 survey by the African Food Security Urban Network (AFSUN) of low-income neighbourhoods found that 25% of households in the poorer areas of the city received income from informal activity.[5]

In Southern Mozambique, the expressions *dumba nengue* (trust your feet) and *dumba kutsutsuma* (run if you can) are used to refer to activities in the informal economy.[6] This terminology clearly reflects the tension that exists between informal traders and law enforcement agents. Compared with other cities in the region, however, Maputo has traditionally adopted a more tolerant approach to the informal economy.[7] Policy interventions aim to discourage informality through registration and formalization rather than by eradication and punishment. Two main strategies have been pursued by the municipal government. First, formal urban markets have been established and existing informal markets have been upgraded and vendors now pay rent for stands. When Xikhelene market was upgraded, all trading on the streets around the old market was eliminated.[8] Second, a simplified tax system was introduced in 2008 that requires traders to pay business tax either as a lump sum or as a percentage of turnover.[9] This initiative has been hampered by low uptake and strong resistance from the informal traders.

ICBT (Informal Cross Border Trade) entrepreneurs operating in Mozambique's informal economy can generally be classified into three groups. The first consists of entrepreneurs who buy and sell goods within Mozambique. A second group comprises entrepreneurs who conduct their business in Mozambique and at least one other country (usually South Africa but also Swaziland and Zimbabwe), buying goods in one country for sale in the other.[10] The third group is primarily involved in the buying and transportation of goods to Mozambique where they sell to informal traders in the marketplaces. All three groups are involved, in one capacity or another, in the informal cross-border trade in goods.

For many years, cross-border trading was confined to those who lived in the border regions of Mozambique. However, it now involves people from virtually every region of the country. This was a direct outcome of the economic and political instability generated by the Mozambican civil war. As the president of the Cross-Border Trade Association recalled:

> *During the civil war, since the cities were starving and women did not have anything to feed their children, they decided to confront bullets and travelled to neighbouring countries just to buy bread and milk, firstly into Swaziland as there were border facilities and later, after the demise of apartheid, they started to go to South Africa. Women took advantage of these crossings and started their businesses. Most of them started with an amount less than $50.*[11]

In the 1990s, a distinguishing feature of informal cross-border trade with South Africa was its undocumented character. Most of the participants did not have passports, and if they did, they could not afford the visa fees. Some were able to make connections with bus crew members to help them cross the border illegally, while others made use of the *marehane*, that is, border crossing facilitators with connections with immigration officers, frontier guards and customs officers.

Mozambique's informal cross-border trade has traditionally been dominated by women.[12] In the late 1990s and early 2000s, female cross-border traders became important players in the Mozambican economy, particularly in the supply of food as well as non-agricultural products such as electrical goods and building materials.[13] A SAMP border monitoring study in Mozambique in 2006-2007 showed that women made up 71% of the total number of cross-border traders.[14] A significant feature of the post-2000 cross-border trade from Mozambique was its diversity. A number of Mozambican traders (37%) said they also traded between Swaziland and Mozambique, buying goods in Swaziland to sell in Maputo.[15] Those travelling to South Africa to buy goods for resale tended to gravitate towards Johannesburg and Durban, while the rest travelled to towns in the neighbouring province of Mpumalanga.[16]

Cross-border trade from Mozambique in the 2000s became important for job creation. Besides being a source of livelihood to the participants, it generated employment in Mozambique. One study showed that over 60% of the Mozambican cross-border traders employed people in their businesses.[17] Another important feature of post-2000 cross-border trade was the growing number of people travelling to South Africa with valid travel documents. The majority of the cross-border traders held valid South African visas.[18] Circulatory movements became more common with as many as 70% of the traders travelling to South Africa for business purposes at least once a week.[19] These circulatory movements were partly a product of the creation of the Maputo Corridor Spatial Development Initiative (SDI) that led to the development of the toll road between Witbank and Maputo and an improved border post at Lebombo.[20] However, others see the Maputo Corridor SDI as a project for large capital and exports rather than an initiative supporting the activities of small-scale traders.[21]

The informal economy in Mozambique has begun to show greater evidence of self-organization. Two main bodies have emerged in the past two decades. The first, the *Associação dos Operadores e Trabalhadores do Sector Informal* (Association of Informal Sector Operators and Workers or ASSOTSI) was launched in Maputo in November 1998.[22] ASSOTSI was formed as a full affiliate of Mozambique's trade union federation, OTM, and was launched to try to stop police harassment of informal traders. By 2006, the association had nearly 5,000 paid-up members operating in 59 markets.[23] The number currently stands at more than 40,000.[24] The second organization, the Association of Informal Sector Traders and Importers, better known as *Mukhero* (which means 'to carry'), was established in 1999 and legally recognized in 2004.[25] A distinctive feature of the organization is that most (70%) of the *Mukheristas* are Maputo-based women.

This report presents the results of a SAMP survey of informal entrepreneurs connected to cross-border trade in Maputo in 2014. The study, which formed part of the IDRC-funded Growing Informal Cities (GIC) project, sought to enhance the evidence base on the links between migration and informal entrepreneurship in Southern African cities and to examine the implications for municipal, national and regional policy. An understanding of the conditions in which cross-border traders operate and their contribution to the local economy can play an important role in the development of a policy framework for facilitating migrant entrepreneurship in Mozambique and other countries within the region.

## RESEARCH METHODOLOGY

The research methodology for this study of informal entrepreneurs was planned in GIC partner meetings in Cape Town. A survey instrument was developed for administration to cross-border entrepreneurs in Harare, Johannesburg and Maputo. The questionnaire was administered to a sample of 403 informal traders in seven Maputo markets. The sample was divided into three entrepreneurial categories (Table 1):

- Category A: Mozambican traders who travel to and from Johannesburg as part of their business, buying goods in South Africa and selling them in Maputo. A total of 243 of these cross-border traders were included in the sample.

- Category B: Mozambican traders who travel to and from Johannesburg, buying goods in South Africa and supplying other informal traders in Maputo. These traders supply vendors in the markets and others such as Indian-owned shops. Indian traders tend to avoid crossing borders themselves because of the harassment they say they experience from customs officials who see them as wealthy and willing to pay bribes. A total of 55 Category B traders were included in the sample.

- Category C: Mozambican informal traders who do not travel, but buy goods from cross-border traders for resale. A total of 99 Category C traders were included in the sample.

In sum, 61% of the sample were cross-border traders who travel to and from South Africa as part of their business, 14% were trader intermediaries who travel to South Africa to buy goods and sell to other traders on return, and 29% did not cross international borders but obtained their goods from those who did.

Table 1: Market Location and Types of Trader

| Markets | No. of interviews | A | B | C |
|---|---|---|---|---|
| Estrela Vermelha | 59 | 37 | 9 | 13 |
| Mandela | 40 | 23 | 6 | 11 |
| Xiquelene | 67 | 42 | 9 | 16 |
| Malanga e Fajardo | 79 | 48 | 13 | 18 |
| Praça de Touros | 28 | 13 | 7 | 8 |
| Xipamanine | 92 | 58 | 11 | 23 |
| Museu | 38 | 22 | 6 | 10 |
| Total | 403 | 243 | 61 | 99 |

The sampling procedure tried to capture the range of products sold in different markets as the markets are getting more specialized, primarily because of their geographical location and potential customer base. Most customers who buy at Museu Market, for example, come from the relatively wealthy areas of Museu, Polana and Sommerschield, while people who buy at Xiquelene mainly come from poor wards. Foodstuffs are the primary product at Xiquelene while Museu's main products are alcohol and cigarettes. Praça de Touros market is situated in one of the busiest areas of Maputo and mainly caters to vehicle owners who need spare parts. It also has a car-repair garage. Estrela Vermelha market, known as Red Star Shopping Centre, sells a variety of goods including household furniture, alcohol and cigarettes. This market is located between Central and Alto Mae wards, and suburbs such as Mafalala, and serves people in both middle- and low-income brackets.

Not all of the goods in the markets come from South Africa. As well as locally sourced agricultural products, goods come from as far afield as Europe and South America. Frozen chicken from Brazil is a common sight in many of the markets.[26] There is also a major trade in imported second-hand clothes (Table 2). At the Xipamanine market in Maputo, for instance, hundreds of traders sell second-hand clothing from Australia, Europe and North America.[27] Many of the clothes that reach Xipamanine are of low quality and, according to one researcher, neither improve the lives of the vendors nor the consumers, an outcome that he terms "clothing poverty."[28]

Table 2: Main Products Sold by Market

| Market | Main products sold |
|---|---|
| Estrela Vermelha | Alcohol, cigarettes, vehicle spare parts, electronics, clothing and household furniture |
| Museu | Alcohol and cigarettes |
| Mandela | Vegetables, alcohol and cigarettes |
| Praça de Touros | Vehicle spare parts |
| Zimpeto | Vegetables, groceries and household furniture |
| Xipamanine | Meat, groceries, vegetables, new and second-hand clothing, *capulanas* (sarongs), live animals such as goats, chicken and ducks and medicine prescribed by traditional doctors |
| Malanga | Groceries, vegetables and textiles including *capulanas* |
| Xiquelene | Construction material, household furniture, clothing, groceries, fruit, vegetables and textiles |
| Malanga and Fajardo | Groceries and vegetables |

Source: Interviews with president of Cross-Border Trade Association and market managers (August to December 2014).

A number of qualitative methods were used to collect additional information for the study. Four focus group discussions were conducted with traders from the following markets: Xiquelene, Zimpeto, Malanga and Museu. Key informant interviews were conducted with different government, private sector and international organization stakeholders with an interest in the informal economy. Among the issues covered in the interviews were the history of cross-border trade in the country, the role of cross-border trade in economic development, legislation governing the informal economy, and the challenges faced by cross-border traders.

## PROFILE OF RESPONDENTS

There is a general perception that cross-border trading in Mozambique is predominantly undertaken by women, while men tend to stay at home and sell products brought into the country by women.[29] The predominance of women in cross-border trade has been attributed to their long experience in crossing borders dating back to the early days of Mozambique's 16-year civil war; their business acumen; their familiarity with managers of wholesale storehouses in Johannesburg; and the fact that they find it more difficult than men to access formal employment.[30] Male respondents claimed that females are better equipped to deal with customs officials and have strategies for avoiding paying import duties; that they themselves viewed trading as more of a hobby or a way to generate extra income; and that they have greater access to jobs in the formal sector. However, some studies have shown growing participation of men in Mozambican informal cross-border trade over time.[31] In this study, 56% of those interviewed were men (Table 3). It is likely that the profile of the respondents would have weighted more heavily in favour of women if the study had been conducted at the border. Women tend to find it easier to be involved in cross-border trade and leave the marketing of the products to either their partners or sons.[32]

Table 3: Gender Profile of Traders

| | Cross-border traders (%) | Cross-border trader intermediaries (%) | Non-cross-border traders (%) | Total (%) |
|---|---|---|---|---|
| Male | 35.1 | 6.5 | 14.9 | 56.5 |
| Female | 26.3 | 7.2 | 10.0 | 43.5 |
| Total | 61.4 | 13.7 | 24.9 | 100.0 |
| N=402 | | | | |

Racially, the overwhelming majority of the respondents (99%) were Black, while a minority were of mixed race, Indian or Asian (Table 4). The mean age of the sample was 37 years with 42% aged between 30 and 39 and 28% between 40 and 49. Around 10% were over the age of 50, and the oldest respondent was 78. Participation by young people in the trade was relatively limited with only 20% under the age of 30. Across all the categories, individuals aged between 20 and 49 made up more than 85% of the total participants.

Table 4: Race and Age Profile of Traders

| | Cross-border traders (%) | Cross-border trader intermediaries (%) | Non-cross-border traders (%) | Total |
|---|---|---|---|---|
| **Race (N=391)** | | | | |
| Black | 98.3 | 98.2 | 100.0 | 98.7 |
| Mixed race | 0.4 | 1.8 | 0.0 | 0.5 |
| Indian | 0.4 | 0.0 | 0.0 | 0.3 |
| Other Asian | 0.4 | 0.0 | 0.0 | 0.3 |
| Other race | 0.4 | 0.0 | 0.0 | 0.3 |
| **Age (N=395)** | | | | |
| Below 20 | 0.0 | 0.0 | 1.0 | 0.3 |
| 20-29 | 18.9 | 16.7 | 28.6 | 21.0 |
| 30-39 | 42.8 | 44.4 | 36.7 | 41.5 |
| 40-49 | 29.6 | 29.6 | 23.5 | 28.1 |
| 50-59 | 6.2 | 7.4 | 9.2 | 7.1 |
| 60-69 | 2.1 | 1.9 | 0.0 | 1.5 |
| 70 and above | 0.4 | 0.0 | 1.0 | 0.5 |

The vast majority of the respondents (92%) were Mozambican-born (Table 5). However, the survey found several immigrant traders from countries such as Nigeria (6%), India, Burundi, Ivory Coast, Guinea (Conakry), Malawi, Namibia, Rwanda, Somalia and Uganda. Of the foreign-born traders interviewed in the survey, slightly more than half (52%) travel to Johannesburg to buy goods for resale in Mozambique. The rest obtain their goods from cross-border traders. In contrast to this, 75% of Mozambicans source their goods directly from South Africa, which suggests that foreign traders cannot or prefer not to go to South Africa to buy their goods. Whatever the reasons, they do face structural barriers that hinder them from fully participating in cross-border trading and, consequently, they rely on Mozambican intermediaries to supply them with goods.

Table 5: Country of Birth of Traders

| | Cross-border traders (%) | Cross-border trader intermediaries (%) | Non-cross-border traders (%) | Total (%) |
|---|---|---|---|---|
| Mozambique | 57.0 | 12.8 | 22.0 | 91.8 |
| Nigeria | 2.8 | 0.8 | 2.3 | 5.8 |
| India | 0.5 | 0.0 | 0.0 | 0.5 |
| Burundi | 0.0 | 0.0 | 0.2 | 0.3 |
| Cote D'Ivoire | 0.0 | 0.3 | 0.0 | 0.3 |
| Guinea (Conakry) | 0.3 | 0.0 | 0.0 | 0.3 |
| Malawi | 0.3 | 0.0 | 0.0 | 0.3 |
| Namibia | 0.3 | 0.0 | 0.0 | 0.3 |
| Rwanda | 0.0 | 0.0 | 0.3 | 0.3 |
| Somalia | 0.3 | 0.0 | 0.0 | 0.3 |
| Uganda | 0.0 | 0.0 | 0.2 | 0.3 |
| Total | 61.3 | 13.8 | 25.0 | 100.0 |
| N=400 | | | | |

Involvement in the informal economy is usually associated with low levels of educational attainment. As many as 75% of the respondents had less than high school qualifications, and fewer than 2% had completed an undergraduate degree (Figure 1). Interestingly, traders who do not travel to Johannesburg themselves but obtain goods from cross-border traders, had the highest level of education, with 28% having completed at least high school compared to 22% of the cross-border traders who travel to Johannesburg as part of their business and 16% of the intermediaries who supply goods to non-cross-border traders in Maputo.

In understanding how household structure affects participation in the business of informal trade, marital status needs to be considered. For example, are the traders independent operators looking out for themselves, or heads of households that depend on them for a livelihood, or are they just contributing to household income? Given that this business can require cross-border traders to be away from the household for several days at a time, there was an expectation that it might be dominated by single, widowed and divorced people. However, the survey found that only 29% were single (which tallies with the more mature age profile of the entrepreneurs) and 6% were divorced or widowed. Of the rest, 38% were married or in a common law relationship and a further 26% were co-habiting (Figure 2).

Figure 1: Highest Level of Education of Traders

Figure 2: Marital Status of Traders

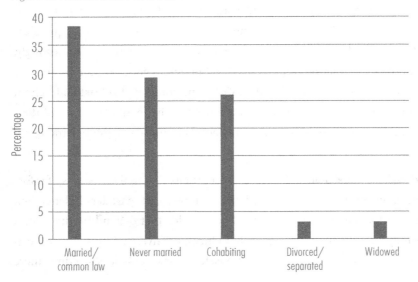

More than half of the respondents (52%) came from nuclear households (defined as a family made up of husband/male partner and wife/female partner with or without children) (Figure 3). About 16% came from male-centred households, where there is no wife/female partner in the household and 13% were from female-centred households. Another 11% were from extended households, while only 7% lived alone. An AFSUN survey in Maputo in 2008/2009 showed that the majority of residents in the poorer areas of the city came from extended households, even though female-centred and nuclear households were also common.[33] This seems to suggest an interesting variation in patterns of participation by type of household. In total, 66% of households are male-headed nuclear and extended family households. These households constitute 63% of the traders' households (although why extended families are far less likely to participate than nuclear families is unclear). The major difference is in female-centred household participation where these households constitute 27% of all households but only supply 13% of traders, suggesting that these household heads are inhibited from participation because they cannot leave their children. Male-centred households appear not to have a problem, with 8% of the total number of households supplying 16% of the traders.

Figure 3: Household Type of ICBT Traders

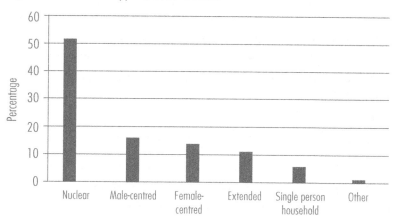

## ENTREPRENEURIAL MOTIVATION

An examination of reasons why the traders established a cross-border trading business is useful in understanding whether they have entrepreneurial motivations or are mere survivalists forced by necessity to trade in the informal economy. To identify the importance of various "entrepreneurial triggers", the survey used an adapted schema from the entrepreneurship literature which asked the respondents to rank the importance of various factors on a motivation scale ranging from 1 (no importance) to 5 (extremely important). These factors were then grouped into four types: financial benefits/security; market/business opportunities; intrinsic/personal rewards; and building human/social/financial capital.

As a group, financial benefits/security motivations were the most important factors and building human/social/financial capital motivations the least (Table 6). The most important financial benefits/security related factors (and the most important factors overall) included the need to give the family greater financial security (mean score of 3.8) and the need for more money just to survive (3.7). It appears that survivalist motivations were greater among non-cross-border traders (3.9) than cross-border traders (3.6).

Market/business related factors scored almost as high as the main survivalist factors. Here, wanting to run one's own business scored 3.6, followed by wanting to expand an existing business (3.5), getting involved in cross-border trading in order to grow one's business (also 3.5) and having a good idea for a product to sell in Mozambique (3.1). Notably, the market/business related factors that drove the cross-border traders into this activity relate more to the opportunities available in Mozambique than in South Africa.

Intrinsic/personal rewards were less important than economic factors. These factors are generally associated with an entrepreneurial personality. The factors cited most by the traders included the desire to do something new and challenging (3.2) and the desire to learn new skills (3.0). By way of comparison, migrant entrepreneurs in the informal economy in Cape Town scored much higher on each of these factors, suggesting a greater degree of entrepreneurial motivation among migrants to that South African city.[34] Intrinsic factors of low importance include enjoying taking risks (2.2) and wanting to compete with others and be the best (2.1).

Finally, factors relating to building human/social/financial capital were generally unimportant entrepreneurial motivators, with the exception of a general desire to contribute to the development of Mozambique (2.9). This desire was greater among cross-border traders (3.0) than cross-border trade intermediaries (2.5). This suggests that, while the state may not recognize their importance or support their activities, cross-border traders do have a broader sense of the developmental value of their activities. This, at least, should prompt a re-examination of the ways in which a supportive policy environment could be created.

Table 6: Entrepreneurial Motivation

| Factor | Cross-border traders | Cross-border trader inter-mediaries | Non-cross-border traders | Mean score |
|---|---|---|---|---|
| **Financial benefits/security** | | | | |
| I wanted to give my family greater financial security | 3.8 | 3.8 | 3.6 | 3.8 |
| I needed more money just to survive | 3.6 | 3.7 | 3.9 | 3.7 |
| I was unemployed and unable to find a job | 2.9 | 3.0 | 3.1 | 3.0 |
| I wanted to make more money to send to my family | 2.4 | 2.5 | 2.3 | 2.4 |
| I had a job but it did not pay enough | 2.1 | 2.4 | 1.9 | 2.1 |
| I had a job but it did not suit my qualifications and experience | 1.9 | 2.1 | 1.9 | 1.9 |
| **Market/business opportunities** | | | | |
| I have always wanted to run my own business | 3.6 | 3.6 | 3.7 | 3.6 |
| I wanted to expand my business | 3.5 | 3.3 | 3.4 | 3.5 |
| I started cross-border trading to grow my business | 3.7 | 3.3 | 3.2 | 3.5 |
| I had a good idea for a product to sell to people | 3.2 | 3.0 | 3.0 | 3.1 |
| There were shortages of certain goods | 3.1 | 2.7 | 2.8 | 3.0 |
| I had a good idea for a product to sell to people from my home country in South Africa | 1.9 | 1.9 | 2.0 | 1.9 |
| I had a good idea for a product to sell in South Africa | 1.8 | 1.5 | 1.8 | 1.7 |
| **Intrinsic/Personal rewards** | | | | |
| I wanted to do something new and challenging | 3.2 | 3.0 | 3.2 | 3.2 |
| I like to learn new skills | 3.1 | 2.7 | 2.9 | 3.0 |
| I like to challenge myself | 3.0 | 2.6 | 2.8 | 2.9 |
| I wanted more control over my own time/to be my own boss | 3.0 | 2.6 | 2.9 | 2.9 |
| I have the right personality to be involved in cross-border trade | 3.0 | 2.2 | 2.3 | 2.8 |
| I enjoy taking risks | 2.1 | 2.1 | 2.3 | 2.2 |
| I wanted to compete with others and be the best | 2.1 | 2.0 | 2.1 | 2.1 |
| **Human, social and financial capital** | | | | |
| I wanted to contribute to the development of my home country | 3.0 | 2.5 | 2.8 | 2.9 |
| I wanted to increase my status in the community | 2.4 | 2.4 | 2.3 | 2.4 |
| I wanted to provide employment for members of my family | 2.4 | 2.4 | 2.4 | 2.4 |

| | | | | |
|---|---|---|---|---|
| My family members have always been involved in cross-border trade | 2.2 | 2.1 | 2.2 | 2.2 |
| I wanted to provide employment for other people | 2.1 | 2.1 | 2.3 | 2.2 |
| Support and help in starting my business was available from family members | 2.1 | 2.1 | 2.1 | 2.1 |
| I decided to go into business in partnership with others | 2.2 | 1.9 | 2.2 | 2.1 |
| Support and help in starting my business was available from other traders | 2.0 | 1.6 | 1.8 | 1.9 |

# BUSINESS START-UP AND OWNERSHIP

## ENTRY INTO ICBT

There is an assumption in the literature that many informal entrepreneurs are "pushed" into participation by unemployment. However, only 26% of the respondents were unemployed before they started their business. Another 19% had been students (Table 7). Around 30% had been employed, primarily in low-paying jobs such as domestic work (9%), agriculture (5%) and unskilled manual labour (3%). Less than 5% had occupied skilled or semi-skilled positions. The rest were already employed (8%) or self-employed (17%) in the informal economy in another enterprise.

The majority of the entrepreneurs involved in ICBT had been in the business for many years. As many as 43% had established their businesses before 2000 and another 41% had done so between 2000 and 2010. Less than 20% had set up shop in the last five years, which may suggest that entry into a highly competitive business is becoming more difficult. The survey also showed that most of the entrepreneurs began their business activities as vendors and only later moved into cross-border trading. So, while over 40% had started their businesses before 2000, only 21% were engaged in ICBT at that time (Figure 4). Conversely, while 57% established their businesses after 2000, the proportion who started ICBT activities during this period was close to 80%. This indicates that most ICBT traders are post-2000 entrants to that market, a direct result of various economic factors and market opportunities. Factors of relevance include the devastating floods of 2000, which impacted on many households; the lifting of South African visa restrictions in 2005; and the strengthening of the metical in comparison to the rand. However, in 2008 (according to interviewees), people feared entering South Africa because of xenophobic attacks.

Table 7: Occupation Prior to Starting the Business

| | No. | % |
|---|---|---|
| Unemployed/job seeker | 105 | 26.3 |
| Scholar/student | 76 | 19.0 |
| Operated informal sector business based only in Mozambique | 68 | 17.0 |
| Domestic worker | 37 | 9.3 |
| Employed by someone in the informal economy | 30 | 7.5 |
| Agricultural worker | 19 | 4.8 |
| Manual worker (unskilled) | 12 | 3.0 |
| Businessman/woman formal sector (self-employed) | 11 | 2.8 |
| Manual worker (skilled) | 7 | 1.8 |
| Office worker | 6 | 1.5 |
| Police/military/security | 3 | 0.8 |
| Teacher | 3 | 0.8 |
| Health worker | 2 | 0.5 |
| Professional (e.g. lawyer, doctor, academic, engineer) | 1 | 0.3 |
| Other occupation | 19 | 4.8 |
| Total | 399 | 100.0 |

Figure 4: Year of Business Start-Up and Entry into Cross-Border Trade

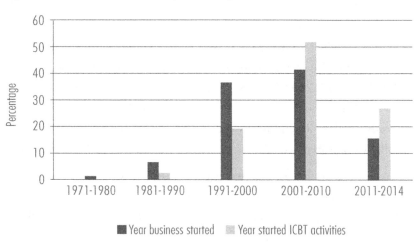

■ Year business started    ▨ Year started ICBT activities

An analysis of the year in which the three categories of business activity were started sheds further light on this question. As many as 49% of the cross-border traders who travel to Johannesburg to buy goods for sale in Mozambique started their business operations before 2000, as against 37% of those who buy goods from cross-border traders and 28% who buy goods from Johannesburg for resale to other traders (Table 8). This suggests that cross-border trading itself is not a new phenomenon but that it has diversified over time with more opportunities for those who sell the goods they buy in Johannesburg to other traders and for those who buy and resell goods without ever having to travel to South Africa.

Table 8: Year in Which Business Established by Type of Activity

| | Cross-border traders (%) | Cross-border trader intermediaries (%) | Non-cross-border traders (%) | Total (%) |
|---|---|---|---|---|
| 1971-1980 | 0.4 | 0.0 | 2.0 | 0.8 |
| 1981-1990 | 7.8 | 3.7 | 3.0 | 6.0 |
| 1991-2000 | 41.2 | 24.1 | 32.3 | 36.7 |
| 2001-2010 | 36.7 | 57.4 | 44.4 | 41.5 |
| 2011-2014 | 13.9 | 14.8 | 18.2 | 15.1 |
| Total | 100.0 | 100.0 | 100.0 | 100.0 |
| N | 245 | 54 | 99 | 398 |

## BUSINESS CAPITAL

The overwhelming majority of the respondents started their businesses from a very low base with three quarters having less than ZAR10,000 to invest (Figure 5). Of these, the majority had between ZAR2,001 and ZAR5,000. Just 15% had invested ZAR20,000 or more. This group was most likely to be cross-border traders (83%) rather than cross-border intermediaries or non-cross-border traders. The non-cross-border traders tended to have the lowest levels of start-up capital with nearly 90% investing ZAR10,000 or less in their businesses.

The sources of capital used to start the business varied but the majority (82%) had used personal savings (Table 9). Other sources of start-up business capital include loans from relatives (used by 33%), bank loans (9%) and loans from informal financial sources (8%). Access to formal sources of business capital was limited, a general reflection of the lack of support given to informal enterprises by formal financial institutions.

Figure 5: Amount of Money Used to Start Business

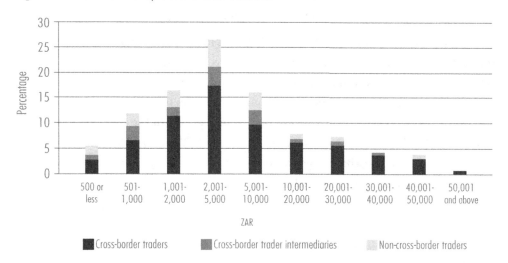

Table 9: Main Sources of Start-Up Capital

|  | No. | % |
| --- | --- | --- |
| Personal savings | 326 | 82.1 |
| Loan from relatives | 129 | 32.5 |
| Bank loan | 34 | 8.6 |
| Loan from informal financial institutions (e.g. *xitique*) | 31 | 7.8 |
| Loan from non-relatives | 11 | 2.8 |
| Business credit (goods on terms) | 8 | 2.0 |
| Loan from micro-finance institution | 6 | 1.5 |
| Usurers/*mashonisa* (money lenders) | 4 | 1.0 |
| Other source | 2 | 0.5 |
| N=397 | | |
| Note: Multiple response question | | |

One recent study showed that nearly 80% of Mozambicans have no access to any sort of banking or microfinance services.[35] Only 12% had access to banking services; 10% to the informal microfinance sector and 1% to formal microfinance services. The survey also showed that 61% of urban and 86% of rural dwellers had no access at all to formal banking services. However, this study of informal entrepreneurs in Maputo found that although most could not get bank loans, as many as 44% had a bank account. However, only 14% said that their enterprise had a separate business account.

To assess whether the traders had an ongoing need for infusions of outside capital, they were asked if they had borrowed money from any source over the previous 12 months. Only 15% had done so. Those who travelled to Johannesburg as part of their business activities were more likely to have done so than those who did not venture across the border (17% versus 7%). Those who had borrowed additional money mostly did so from micro-finance institutions (41%), banks (31%) and from relatives (16%) (Table 10). The loans were used primarily to finance the purchase of goods for sale (62%), improvement of business premises (33%) and purchase of raw materials (19%) (Table 11).

Table 10: Source of Business Loans

| | No. | % |
|---|---|---|
| Micro-finance institution | 24 | 41.4 |
| Bank | 18 | 31.0 |
| Loan from relatives | 9 | 15.5 |
| Usurers/*mashonisa* (money lenders) | 3 | 5.2 |
| Informal financial institution (e.g. *stokvels*) | 2 | 3.4 |
| Loan from other business owners | 1 | 1.7 |
| Loan from government agency | 1 | 1.7 |
| Other source | 1 | 1.7 |
| N=58 | | |
| Note: Multiple response question | | |

Table 11: Use of Business Loans

| | No. | % |
|---|---|---|
| Purchase of goods for sale | 36 | 62.1 |
| Improvement of business premises | 19 | 32.8 |
| Purchase of raw materials | 11 | 19.0 |
| Expansion of the business activity | 2 | 3.4 |
| Rental of market stall | 1 | 1.7 |
| Other use | 3 | 5.2 |
| N=58 | | |
| Note: Multiple response question | | |

Nearly two thirds of those who had borrowed money said that the loan had resulted in an increase in the volume of production (Table 12). As many as 36% said the loan resulted in an increased volume of sales while 22% said the loan resulted in the diversification of production. Clearly, business loans are having a positive impact on the business activities of those cross-border traders who have access to them. By extension, with greater access to business capital, a larger number of cross-border traders would be able to increase the volume of production, increase sales and diversify their business. Only 2% indicated that the loans had led to financial difficulties.

Table 12: Impact of Loans on Business Activity

|  | No. | % |
|---|---|---|
| Increase in the volume of production | 35 | 60.3 |
| Increase in the volume of sales | 21 | 36.2 |
| Diversification of production | 13 | 22.4 |
| Improvement of competitiveness/profitability | 2 | 3.4 |
| Working less time | 1 | 1.7 |
| Caused financial difficulties | 1 | 1.7 |
| Other impact | 4 | 6.9 |
| N=58 | | |
| Note: Multiple response question | | |

The survey also identified some of the barriers to accessing bank loans. Banks in Mozambique usually only lend money to individuals employed in the formal sector because their future earnings serve as a form of guarantee for the loan repayment. Only 24% of the cross-border traders indicated that they had ever applied for a bank loan for their business. Nearly a third (31%) said this was because their business had sufficient capital and they did not need a loan (Table 13). A further 24% were uninterested in getting a loan. The responses from the remaining respondents provide insight into some of the obstacles they face. A significant number (27%) said that they had not applied because the interest rates were too high. A smaller number (8%) said the application procedures were too complicated. Other reasons were that the banks ask for collateral, which they did not have, or that banks would not loan money to people without bank accounts. That said, the success rate for those who had applied for bank loans was surprisingly high at 84%. Moza Bank became the first private bank of Mozambique to give loans to informal traders through the ASSOTSI – Informal Cross-Border Trade Association.[36] The loans are only available to ASSOTSI members who can present a reference from ASSOTSI and a simplified tax return. The loans may be up to one-third of the annual business turnover shown in the tax return, to a maximum loan of MZN100,000.[37]

Table 13: Reasons for Not Applying for a Bank Loan

|  | No. | % |
|---|---|---|
| No need for a loan – have sufficient capital | 76 | 31.0 |
| Interest rates too high | 67 | 27.3 |
| I am not interested in getting a loan from a bank | 59 | 24.1 |
| Application procedures too complicated | 19 | 7.8 |
| Guarantee/collateral asked for is too much | 11 | 4.5 |
| I don't have a bank account | 5 | 2.0 |
| Available loans do not correspond to my needs | 4 | 1.6 |
| Other reason | 4 | 1.6 |
| Total | 245 | 100.0 |

Several government funding schemes are available to small and medium-scale enterprises, but not to businesses in the informal economy:

> The Government of Mozambique through the Ministry of Commerce and Industry has established the Enterprise Competitiveness and Private Sector Development Project, which funds small and middle enterprises for competitiveness. The State does not recognize unlicensed businesses which are run by cross-border traders. To be funded one needs to be licensed. The informal economy is not eligible for funds.[38]

Just over a third of the respondents were aware of the scheme but only 2% had applied, suggesting that they are aware of the ineligibility of informal enterprises for government assistance.

# BUSINESS STRATEGIES

## BUYING PRACTICES

The main objective of the project was to examine the ICBT linkages and flows between Maputo and Johannesburg. Johannesburg was the primary place, and beneficiary, of the purchase of goods by Mozambican traders. On average, the cross-border traders spend 1.52 days in South Africa on each trip. As many as 54% travel to Johannesburg at least once a week, which translates into nearly 80 days per year spent in South Africa. A further 34% travel there at least once a month, which translates into 18 days per year in South Africa (Figure 6).

Figure 6: Frequency of Trips to Johannesburg

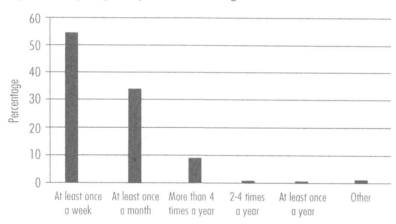

As many as 8% of the respondents indicated that they also buy goods in other places in Gauteng, such as Pretoria and Randfontein (Table 14). More than a third of the respondents purchase goods from other places in South Africa, especially from towns close to the Mozambican border such as Nelspruit, Malelane and Komatipoort (Table 14). These traders are therefore able to conduct their business activities in South Africa and return to Mozambique within the same day. A small number of entrepreneurs (around 12%) also travel to other countries to conduct their business, including Swaziland, China and Dubai (Figure 7). As many as 27% of those who travel to these other countries for business are non-Mozambican nationals, particularly Nigerians.

Table 14: Other Urban Centres Where Goods Purchased

|  | No. | % |
| --- | --- | --- |
| **Do you buy goods from places other than Johannesburg?** | | |
| Yes | 133 | 47.3 |
| No | 148 | 52.7 |
| Total | 281 | 100.0 |
| **Other places in South Africa where goods are bought** | | |
| Nelspruit | 88 | 66.2 |
| Malelane | 51 | 38.3 |
| Durban | 32 | 24.1 |
| Komatipoort | 21 | 15.7 |
| Other places in South Africa | 1 | 0.8 |
| N=133 | | |

Figure 7: Other Countries Where Traders Conduct Their Business

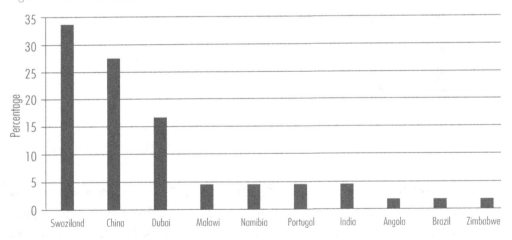

## SELLING PRACTICES

Most of the traders sell the goods from South Africa in Maputo, the capital, while a small number (less than 5%) also sell their goods in other cities such as Xai Xai and Beira. The goods are sold mainly in their own shop in the informal sector (38%) or in their own stall in an informal market (24%) (Table 15). However, there is also evidence of informal-formal sector linkages with 9% selling in their own shop in the formal sector, 8% selling to retailers, 3% to wholesalers and 1% to restaurant owners.

Table 15: Place Where Goods Are Sold

| | No. | % |
|---|---|---|
| Own shop in informal sector | 193 | 37.7 |
| Own stall in informal market | 122 | 23.8 |
| Own shop in formal sector | 45 | 8.8 |
| Retailers and shops | 42 | 8.2 |
| Friends/family/networks | 32 | 6.3 |
| Sellers in informal markets | 22 | 4.3 |
| On the street | 21 | 4.1 |
| Wholesalers | 17 | 3.3 |
| Door to door | 6 | 1.2 |
| From my house | 4 | 0.8 |
| Restaurants | 4 | 0.8 |
| Other places | 3 | 0.6 |
| Total | 512 | 100.0 |
| Note: Multiple response question | | |

## JOB CREATION

A total of 424 other people were employed directly in the businesses interviewed (Figure 8). Around half (51%) provide employment to others, or an average of 2.1 jobs per business. A significant proportion of the traders employ more than one person: 27% of those providing employment had two employees, 10% had three employees and 5% had four or more.

There was a major difference in the employment practices between those who travel to South Africa and those who do not (58% versus 31% providing jobs). This confirms that many cross-border traders prefer to focus on their cross-border activities and employ others to sell the goods on their behalf in Maputo. Non-family members made up 69% of the paid employees, and the rest were family members, with a total of eight employees below the age of 18. Some 71% of the employees were men, confirming that there is an explicit focus on male employment in the businesses supported by ICBT. This seems to support our earlier observation that men prefer not to cross borders but are employed by women in the sale of goods in Mozambique.

Figure 8: Employment by Traders

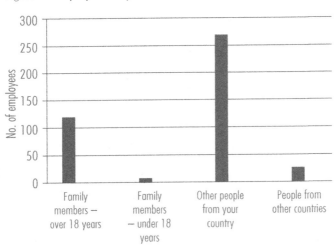

The involvement of children in the informal economy is a controversial issue. Some regard their involvement as an essential part of household survival strategy.[39] Others view it as child labour that limits the proper development of children and should therefore be eliminated.[40] The survey found that 16% of enterprises involve children in their business in different capacities. Participation was higher among children of cross-border traders (20%) than non-cross-border traders (7%). Among those who involve their children, 53% said their children help them to sell goods, 43% sometimes ask their children to look after the stall and 5% involve them in other ways.

## PARTICIPATION IN TRADER ORGANIZATIONS

Participation in trader organizations can potentially have a positive impact on a business. The greatest level of participation among the traders was in *xitique* (money/savings clubs) (at 41%) where they have access to business finance at concessionary rates (Table 16). This informal banking system is not used, on the whole, to bankroll business start-up. Rather, it is a source of funds for family emergencies and can also be drawn on for purchase of goods and stock. Participation in organized traders' associations was low, with only 6% of the traders indicating membership of these organizations. Participation in church associations and burial societies was also limited. More than half of the respondents said they did not participate in any type of organization.

Table 16: Participate in Organisation That Helps Business?

| | Yes | | No | |
|---|---|---|---|---|
| | No. | % | No. | % |
| *Xitique* (money/savings club) | 159 | 40.9 | 230 | 59.1 |
| Traders' association | 25 | 6.4 | 364 | 93.6 |
| Church association | 9 | 2.3 | 380 | 97.7 |
| Burial society | 5 | 1.3 | 384 | 98.7 |
| Do not participate in any organization | 215 | 55.3 | 174 | 44.7 |
| N=389 | | | | |

## BUSINESS PROFITABILITY

Participation in cross-border trading is sometimes viewed as a part-time activity to supplement income from other sources. The overwhelming majority of respondents (90%) have no other income-generating activity and rely solely on their ICBT-supported business for survival (Table 17). Cross-border traders are a little more likely than intermediaries and non-cross-border traders to have other income sources but the overall percentage is still small. Additional income sources included part-time/casual work, other informal businesses and rentals.

Table 17: Other Income-Generating Activities

| | No. | % |
|---|---|---|
| Cross-border traders | 33 | 13.4 |
| Cross-border trader intermediaries | 4 | 7.3 |
| Non-cross-border traders | 5 | 5.1 |
| Total | 42 | 10.5 |

Discussions on informal entrepreneurship have focused on whether the sector can create viable enterprises that can provide decent incomes to the participants. In other words, can cross-border traders generate incomes comparable to formal sector jobs? First, the traders generate an average of ZAR21,838 per month in total sales and a profit of ZAR7,087 per month (Table 18). Cross-border traders who travel to Johannesburg as part of their business activities are likely to generate more monthly sales and profit compared to non-cross-border traders or cross-border trader intermediaries.

Table 18: Total Monthly Sales and Profit

|  | Mean monthly sales (ZAR) | Mean monthly profit (ZAR) |
|---|---|---|
| Cross-border traders | 25,639.89 | 8,169.68 |
| Cross-border trader intermediaries | 11,098.04 | 6,101.39 |
| Non-cross-border traders | 16,416.67 | 5,095.15 |
| Total average | 21,838.28 | 7,086.82 |

Cross-border entrepreneurial activity is certainly financially beneficial to the participants. Nearly two thirds (64%) said that their income status had increased compared to the period before they started their business and only 6% said it had decreased (Figure 9). Another 26% said that their income was variable, going up and down according to market conditions. The greatest improvement was reported by the cross-border traders.

Figure 9: Comparison of Present and Previous Income Status

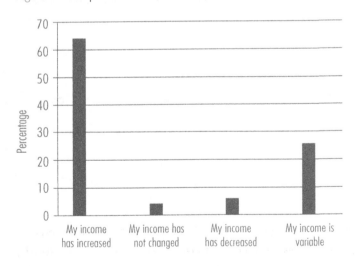

The profits generated from informal business play an important role in meeting personal (79%) and family (77%) needs (Table 19). A quarter of respondents were investing the proceeds in education of family members, more than the proportion re-investing income in the business itself (only 19%). A third said that profits are being saved for future use. Just under 10% send money outside Mozambique as remittances either to support the needs of their family members or for investment in business. Of those sending remittances outside Mozambique, 52% are Mozambicans while the rest are non-nationals (mainly Nigerians).

Table 19: Use of Business Profits

|  | No. | % |
|---|---|---|
| Spent on myself | 298 | 79.3 |
| Spent on family needs in Mozambique | 289 | 76.9 |
| Personal savings | 121 | 32.2 |
| Education | 99 | 26.3 |
| Re-investment in business in Mozambique | 72 | 19.1 |
| Remittances for family needs | 27 | 7.2 |
| Retirement fund | 26 | 6.9 |
| Re-investment in business outside Mozambique | 6 | 1.6 |
| Other | 2 | 0.5 |
| N=376 | | |
| Note: Multiple response question | | |

## CONTRIBUTIONS TO THE SOUTH AFRICAN ECONOMY

Who benefits most in South Africa from the purchasing behaviour of Mozambican cross-border entrepreneurs? This section examines the activities of those cross-border traders who travel to South Africa and seeks to identify the South African beneficiaries of ICBT.[41] This is an important topic given the xenophobia in South Africa that affects the operations of all non-South African participants in the informal economy there.[42] First, ICBT between South Africa and Mozambique contributes to South Africa's massive trade surplus with Mozambique by exporting South African goods and importing far less from Mozambique. Only 5% of the traders sell products from Mozambique in South Africa (including cigarettes, fabric/capulana, fresh fruit and vegetables, and alcohol). Most of these products are sold through personal networks, but also to wholesalers and informal vendors.

Second, a wide variety of outlets in South Africa benefit from patronage by Mozambican traders including wholesalers, supermarkets, small retailers (formal and informal), factories, farms and fresh produce markets. Easily the most important beneficiaries of Mozambican patronage are South African wholesalers (used by 48%). Other important sources of goods for the traders include the Johannesburg Fresh Produce Market (21%), supermarkets (16%), manufacturers (16%) and small shops or retailers either in a mall (15%) or outside a mall (9%) (Table 20). Chinese shops are also popular with the cross-border traders with 19% buying goods from the China Mall and 11% buying goods from other Chinese-run malls.

Table 20: Source of Goods in South Africa

|  | % |
| --- | --- |
| Wholesalers | 48.4 |
| City Deep/Johannesburg Fresh Produce Market | 20.7 |
| China Mall | 18.4 |
| Supermarkets | 16.4 |
| Manufacturer/factories | 15.8 |
| Small shops/retailers (in a mall) | 14.8 |
| Other Chinese-run mall | 10.5 |
| Small shops/retailers (not in a mall) | 8.9 |
| Direct from farmers | 5.3 |
| Other fresh produce markets | 4.9 |
| Informal sector producer/retailer | 3.6 |
| Oriental Plaza | 1.0 |
| Other place | 2.3 |
| N=304 | |
| Note: Multiple response question | |

The goods bought in South Africa can be grouped into five main categories: food and beverages, household/home goods, personal goods, electrical goods and miscellaneous (Table 21). In the first category of food and beverages, the most common items were cooking oil (purchased by 22% on their last visit), eggs (20%), alcohol (20%), mealie meal (18%) and fresh fruit and vegetables (18%). The most popular household/home goods were household products (26%) and bedding material such as blankets and duvets (8%). Personal goods were dominated by new clothing and footwear (19%), while electronics and cellphones and phone accessories were the most popular electrical goods bought in South Africa.

Table 21: Kind of Goods Usually Bought in South Africa

|  | No . | % |
|---|---|---|
| **Food and beverages** | | |
| Cooking oil | 68 | 22.4 |
| Eggs | 61 | 20.1 |
| Alcohol | 61 | 20.1 |
| Mealie meal | 55 | 18.1 |
| Fresh produce (fruits and vegetables) | 55 | 18.1 |
| Sugar | 48 | 15.8 |
| Milk (fresh, sour) | 45 | 14.8 |
| Tea/coffee | 40 | 13.2 |
| Tinned/canned fruits and vegetables | 38 | 12.5 |
| Meat (fresh, frozen) | 26 | 8.6 |
| Snacks (chips, Nik Naks etc.) | 23 | 7.6 |
| Rice and pasta (spaghetti, macaroni) | 19 | 6.3 |
| Confectionary (sweets, cakes, chocolates) | 8 | 2.6 |
| Bread | 2 | 0.7 |
| Fish (fresh, frozen) | 2 | 0.7 |
| **Household goods** | | |
| Household products | 78 | 25.7 |
| Bedding (blankets/duvets etc) | 24 | 7.9 |
| Plastic goods | 15 | 4.9 |
| Building materials | 8 | 2.6 |
| Furniture | 7 | 2.3 |
| Beds and mattresses | 6 | 2.0 |
| Fabric/*capulana* | 4 | 1.3 |
| **Personal goods** | | |
| New clothing and footwear | 57 | 18.8 |
| Toiletries and cosmetics | 25 | 8.2 |
| Accessories (bags, sunglasses etc.) | 21 | 6.9 |
| Second-hand clothing and footwear | 4 | 1.3 |
| Cigarettes | 4 | 1.3 |
| Books | 1 | 0.3 |

| Electrical goods | | |
|---|---|---|
| Electronics | 31 | 10.2 |
| Cellphones/phone accessories | 30 | 9.9 |
| Computers/computer accessories | 6 | 2.0 |
| Music/CDs/DVDs | 6 | 2.0 |
| Miscellaneous goods | | |
| Car parts | 41 | 13.5 |
| Spare parts and raw materials | 12 | 3.9 |
| Hardware/tools | 9 | 3.0 |
| Traditional medicine | 6 | 2.0 |
| N=304 | | |
| Note: Multiple response question | | |

A third beneficiary of the presence of the Mozambican traders is the South African Treasury. Most of the prices that the traders pay for their goods include VAT, although VAT refunds can be claimed as these goods are not consumed within South Africa. VAT refunds ensure that the traders are not double taxed through paying VAT in South Africa and customs duty at the border. On their last trip to South Africa, however, only 55% of traders had claimed the refunds. Of the 45% who did not claim VAT, nearly half said they did not know the procedure and 36% that the procedure takes too long. In focus group discussions it emerged that one of the reasons was that bus drivers did not want to spend time at the border while customs officials searched for goods. This makes it extremely difficult for the traders using public transport to submit VAT refund claims. Those using taxis or their own vehicles are more likely to claim VAT refunds. While it is advantageous for South Africa if people do not claim these refunds when they leave the country, it is fundamentally unfair to the traders. The Mozambican government and civil society should launch an education campaign aimed at educating the cross-border traders on their rights and the procedures to claim VAT refunds. In addition, the Mozambican government needs to work with its South African counterparts to clear the bureaucratic bottlenecks related to claiming VAT refunds.

Fourth, ICBT traders spent money on transportation, accommodation and food when in South Africa. About 37% usually stay in paid accommodation including rented rooms, hotels, guesthouses and B&Bs (Table 22). Those who do not pay for accommodation sleep at the bus or train station, sleep on the street, stay with friends and family or sleep in an automobile. Public transport is the most common way for traders to travel to and from

Johannesburg, including buses (used by 43%), trucks (15%), taxis (11%), and trains (1%) (Table 23). Others use private transport including their own vehicles (13%), individually-rented vehicles (11%) and vehicles rented with others (6%) but still pay for petrol and other costs, such as parking, in South Africa.

Table 22: Accommodation in South Africa

|  | No. | % |
|---|---|---|
| **Paid accommodation** | | |
| Rent/rent shared room | 36 | 15.2 |
| Hotel (shared room) | 34 | 14.3 |
| Bed and breakfast/guest house/lodge (own room) | 13 | 5.5 |
| Hotel (own room) | 3 | 1.3 |
| Bed and breakfast/guest house/lodge (shared room) | 2 | 0.8 |
| **Non-paying accommodation** | | |
| Bus or train station | 51 | 21.5 |
| Stay with friends and family | 40 | 16.9 |
| Street | 35 | 14.8 |
| In car or truck | 14 | 5.9 |
| Stay with partner | 9 | 3.8 |
| Total | 237 | 100.0 |

Table 23: Mode of Transport

|  | No. | % |
|---|---|---|
| Bus | 148 | 48.7 |
| Trucks | 50 | 16.4 |
| Own vehicle | 43 | 14.1 |
| Taxi | 37 | 12.2 |
| Rented vehicle | 37 | 12.2 |
| Rent vehicle with friends/rent space in vehicle | 21 | 6.9 |
| Train | 4 | 1.3 |
| Other type of transport | 2 | 0.7 |
| Total | 304 | 100.0 |
| Note: Multiple response question | | |

In terms of the monetary spend in South Africa, the cross-border traders reported spending an average of ZAR14,287 on goods, ZAR1,714 on customs duties, ZAR1,441.21 on transport, ZAR218 on accommodation and ZAR258 on other expenses on their last trip (Figure 10). In total, a trader travelling from Maputo to Johannesburg thus spent approximately ZAR17,900 per trip on business-related costs. This translates to nearly ZAR5.4 million per trip for the entire sample, most of which directly benefits the South African economy (Table 24). The financial contribution of cross-border traders to the South African economy is clearly significant.

Figure 10: Mean Spend by Cross-Border Traders

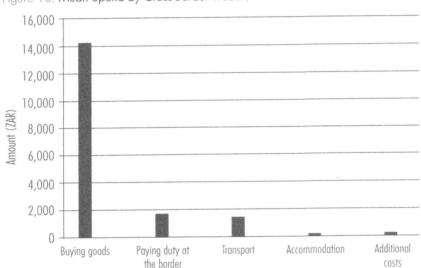

Table 24: Contribution to Local and Regional Economy

| | Buying goods (ZAR) | Paying duty at the border (ZAR) | Transport (ZAR) | Accommodation (ZAR) | Additional costs (ZAR) | Total (ZAR) |
|---|---|---|---|---|---|---|
| Amount per individual | 14,287.21 | 1,714.38 | 1,441.21 | 218.28 | 258.49 | 17,919.57 |
| Total amount for sample | 4,343,311 | 521,171 | 438,127 | 66,357 | 78,580 | 5,447,549 |

# BUSINESS CHALLENGES

## TYPE OF DOCUMENTATION

In general, traders do not have problems with their documentation and immigration status when in South Africa. The introduction of the visa exemption for Mozambicans certainly played a significant role in reducing undocumented migration from Mozambique. The survey results show that just under three-quarters of the respondents (74%) hold visitors' permits when they travel to South Africa (Figure 11). About 15% said they do not need any permits (presumably because they have some kind of residence status in South Africa). A small number have work permits (3%), permanent residence permits (1%) and other permits (3%). Significantly, only 2% travel to South Africa with no official documentation. The vast majority of the Mozambican cross-border traders therefore enter the country using legal channels and there is little evidence to suggest that they use irregular channels.

Figure 11: Type of Documentation When in South Africa

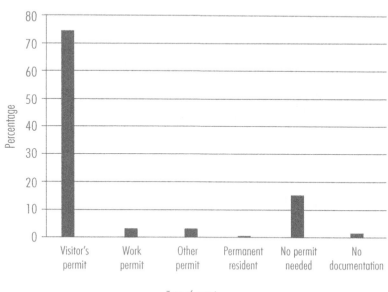

## PROBLEMS CROSSING THE BORDER

The most important border or customs-related problem cited by the cross-border traders was corruption, experienced often or sometimes by 86% of the respondents (Table 25). Corruption leads to a reduction in government customs revenue collection and may also result in a reduction of the profit margins of the cross-border traders, which ultimately reduces prospects for business expansion. Others claimed that the duties that they pay at the border are too high (85% often/sometimes), while long queues, congestion and delays at the border are experienced often/sometimes by 82% of the cross-border traders. Clearly the traders are dissatisfied with the time it takes them to clear customs at the border and there is evidence to suggest that paying bribes can help speed up the process for them. Some of the study participants noted that they use the *magaigai* or intermediaries with experience in dealing with customs officials in an attempt to avoid paying the high duties.

Table 25: Problems Related to Customs and Immigration

| | Often/ some- times (%) | Never (%) |
|---|---|---|
| Too much corruption at border post | 86.0 | 14.0 |
| Duties paid are too high | 85.3 | 14.7 |
| Long queues/congestion/delays at border post | 82.3 | 17.7 |
| Restrictions on import/export of goods (type and volume) | 66.7 | 33.3 |
| Unwarranted confiscation/detention of goods | 65.3 | 34.7 |
| Transport problems/poor road networks/transport prices high | 32.3 | 67.7 |
| Days allowed in destination country are too few | 30.0 | 70.0 |
| Verbal harassment by police, army, border officials of my home country | 19.3 | 80.7 |
| Verbal harassment by South African police, army, border officials | 19.7 | 80.3 |
| Physical harassment/beating/rights violation by South African police, army, border officials | 12.0 | 88.0 |
| Physical harassment/beating/rights violations by police, army, border officials of home country | 11.0 | 89.0 |
| Physical harassment/beating by other people | 8.3 | 91.7 |
| N=300 | | |

Other respondents noted that they experience restrictions on the types and volumes of goods that they can either import or export (experienced often/sometimes by 67% of respondents). During the focus group discussions, one trader noted that "we can import spare vehicles, vegetables, groceries, fruit, meat, furniture, alcohol. The only limitation is related with duties and some do not know the Common Customs Tariff, which is a heavy book to be read."[43] Meanwhile, the president of the Mukhero Association said this about the Common Customs Tariff:

> *Mukheristas get advice from the association about their rights and obligations and some were trained. All the time that the Government updates duties or other related issues the associations are informed. As a matter of fact, before any increase or changes on Common Customs Tariff, the Government calls the associations to inform them, otherwise we block the streets. When the Government of South Africa introduced a new regulation that every crosser should prove they had an amount of ZAR3,000, we felt that was a decision that had to be discussed between the two governments. We were concerned about security and not every trader carries that amount of money. South Africans should understand that we bring money to them and we are no longer poor as it was in the past during the civil war.*[44]

Others cited the unwarranted confiscation/detention of goods at the border (56% often/ sometimes). A focus group participant noted that they are sometimes forced to leave their goods at the border if they fail to reach a reasonable agreement with customs officials. Participants noted that it was not worthwhile trying to get goods back because of the high cost of import duty, especially on goods such as cigarettes and alcohol. The customs department is said to auction confiscated goods.

Even though only a small proportion of the respondents reported cases of harassment and abuse, these are significant enough to warrant attention. Verbal harassment by police, army and border officials had been experienced often/sometimes by the cross-border traders on both the South African (16%) and Mozambican (16%) sides of the border. Physical harassment/beating/violation of human rights by police, army and border officials had also been experienced often/sometimes on both the South African (11%) and Mozambican (10%) sides of the border.

The chair of the Mukhero Association described what happens at the border as a struggle between traders and customs officials:

> *It is a titanic fight as both officers and traders are strong. Traders have their way of fighting and avoiding customs, while customs use their power as official authority, but we do have our own ways of counteracting them. However, this*

*fight ended by the time the cross-border traders realized that the only way of this fight was to meet with the authorities, as well the government did in Rome with RENAMO. Conversation is the only way to avoid death of people, because the authorities were using fire weapons as well as some traders also had weapons.*[45]

## CHALLENGES CONDUCTING BUSINESS

The challenges faced by the traders in their daily operations can be divided into two categories: those experienced while conducting business operations in Mozambique and those encountered when travelling to South Africa for business. In Mozambique, the most common problems related to competition from other traders (65.5%), competition from large retailers or supermarkets (45%), insecurity or problems securing a selling site (43%), conflicts with other traders (35%) and confiscation of merchandise (34%) (Table 26).

Table 26: Challenges in Daily Operations of Business

| | Often/ sometimes (%) | Never (%) |
|---|---|---|
| **In Mozambique** | | |
| Competition from other traders | 65.5 | 34.5 |
| Competition from large retailers or supermarkets | 45.0 | 55.0 |
| Insecurity of selling site/problems securing a selling site when needed | 42.8 | 57.3 |
| Difficulty negotiating with other traders/conflicts among traders | 34.5 | 65.5 |
| Confiscation of goods/difficulty getting merchandise back after it is confiscated | 33.8 | 66.3 |
| Theft of money or goods | 31.5 | 68.5 |
| Harassment by authorities in Mozambique (e.g. police or other officials) | 18.0 | 82.0 |
| No relevant training in accounting, marketing, other business skills | 13.5 | 86.5 |
| Prejudice against my gender | 11.8 | 88.3 |
| **In South Africa** | | |
| Difficulty finding an affordable and safe place to stay | 21.7 | 78.3 |
| Insecurity of selling site/problems securing a selling site | 18.0 | 82.0 |
| Harassment by authorities in South Africa (e.g. police or other officials) | 12.7 | 87.3 |
| Prejudice against my nationality | 12.7 | 87.3 |
| Harassment by South African traders | 9.7 | 90.3 |

Theft of goods is faced by the traders on their way home from South Africa. This is related to renewed conflict in Mozambique where armed opposition party members are said to attack travellers in order to loot their cash and goods. One of the focus group discussion participants noted that:

> Bandits assault the Mukheristas taxis. They use mats with nails to punch the tyres. Then they steal their money. Some Mukheristas do carry a lot of money, sometimes more than R10,000 in one trip. Last year one of our mates was on her way to Johannesburg when the taxi she was travelling in was ambushed near Machado. She lost more than R40,000 cash in the robbery. There were 10 traders in that taxi.[46]

In South Africa, the biggest challenges relate to the difficulty of finding an affordable and safe place to stay in Johannesburg (22% often/sometimes), securing a trading site (18%), prejudice against their nationality (13%), harassment by the police or municipal authorities (13%) and harassment by South African traders (10%).

The study also sought to understand the cross-border traders' experience of xenophobia in South Africa. Nearly one in five of the respondents (19%) noted that their business had been affected by xenophobia a great deal or to some extent (Figure 12). However, as many as 63% said that xenophobia had not affected their business at all. While these findings are encouraging, given the widespread xenophobic attitudes and attacks on informal entrepreneurs, it is likely that Mozambicans are able to avoid the worst forms of victimization by having a legal right to be in the country, by not remaining long and by not competing directly with South African informal businesses.[47]

Finally, the survey asked traders about the ways they are treated while conducting their business activities in both Mozambique and South Africa. Across all but one of the measures, the traders experienced more problems in Mozambique than in South Africa. They have had their business goods looted more often in Mozambique than in South Africa (47% versus 19%) (Table 27). They have been robbed more in Mozambique than in South Africa (39% versus 15%) and assaulted more too (19% versus 12%). In addition, harassment by local authorities was more frequent in Mozambique (11%) than in South Africa (5%), as were incidents of unlawful arrest (6% and 1%, respectively).

In addition, cross-border traders and intermediaries were more likely to experience operational problems in Mozambique than those who buy goods from cross-border traders. For instance, they were likely to have had business goods looted (43%) compared to non-cross-border traders (38%). They were also more likely to report more incidences of harassment by other local traders (9%) compared to 5% for non-cross-border traders. However, non-cross-border traders operating in the informal economy were more likely to have been victims of robbery (40%) and have had business premises destroyed (10%) compared to cross-border traders (33% and 9%, respectively).

Figure 12: Extent to Which Xenophobia Has Affected Business Operations

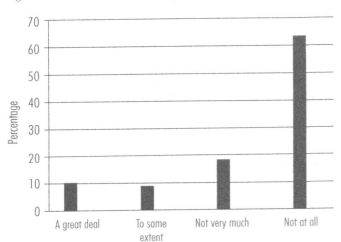

Table 27: Treatment in Mozambique Compared With South Africa

|  | Mozambique (% often/sometimes) | South Africa (% often/sometimes) |
|---|---|---|
| Had business goods looted | 46.7 | 18.9 |
| Been robbed | 38.8 | 15.1 |
| Been assaulted | 18.8 | 12.2 |
| Been harassed by local authorities | 10.8 | 5.1 |
| Had business premises destroyed | 9.9 | 2.7 |
| Been harassed by local traders | 9.2 | 2.9 |
| Failed to access business finance | 8.0 | 3.0 |
| Been arrested unlawfully | 5.6 | 1.1 |
| Lost business to a South African | 0.0 | 1.1 |

Other challenges were also highlighted by traders in the interviews and focus groups:

- The local authorities, and even the national government, do not recognize the contribution of the informal economy to national development. Instead, they view cross-border traders as people who engage in illegal activities. While they argue that street vendors or vendors in stalls and informal markets across the city are not registered and therefore cannot be recognized or supported, the municipality still charges a daily tax of MZN5 for the "right" to trade. Hence, the traders felt that they were not getting the necessary support from the government while they were paying taxes and contributing to employment creation in the country.

- The document governing the entry of goods into Mozambique, the Custom Customs Tariff, is complex and needs to be simplified to make it easier for cross-border traders to understand.

- Business is negatively affected by currency fluctuations.

- The traders sometimes experience difficulties trying to import perishable goods such as meat, beverages, vegetables, fruit and dairy products. The length of time it takes to clear the goods at the border can result in some becoming inedible.

- Obtaining a visitor's permit to enter South Africa requires a passport. But the cost of acquiring a new passport is very high and considering that some of the traders travel to South Africa once a week, renewals are frequently needed.

## CONCLUSION

Cross-border trading has become a way of life for many in Mozambique, geographically encompassing every part of the country and also involving migrants from other countries residing in Mozambique. Cross-border trade in Mozambique is work primarily done by women with men mainly involved in the sale of the products brought back from South Africa. The traders are clearly playing a key role in supplying commodities that are in scarce supply in Mozambique. Even though the sector is an important part of the Mozambican economy, little support is granted to the traders by local and municipal authorities or the private sector. Access to finance remains a major obstacle to business success as neither the government nor private banks provide loans to the traders.

This report has demonstrated the specific roles played by the cross-border traders in the economies of both Mozambique and South Africa. It has shown that cross-border traders contribute to the South African economy through buying goods, as well as paying for accommodation and transport costs. The cross-border traders are directly contributing to the retail, hospitality and transport sectors in South Africa, thereby creating and sustaining jobs in those sectors. In Mozambique, the traders pay import duty for the goods bought in South Africa and they play a significant role in reducing poverty and unemployment in the country. Therefore, the policy environment should encourage rather than discourage the operation of ICBT. A change in attitude of government towards cross-border traders is required as they do contribute to poverty alleviation, and there is a definite need for a forum that involves government and municipal officials and the traders.

There is scope therefore to include the informal traders in Mozambique's poverty alleviation strategy. Although they are regarded as informal, they pay taxes to the local authorities for access to trading sites. They also buy goods in South Africa, some of which are sold to formal retailers, thereby blurring the formal-informal boundary. The informal tag becomes a hindrance when considering the functioning of the Mozambican economy. The traders need to be seen as an essential component of the Mozambican economy because, in their absence, the economy would be very different and poorer than it is today.

## ENDNOTES

1   Jones and Tarp, "Jobs and Welfare in Mozambique"; Nucifora and da Silva, "Rapid Growth and Economic Transformation in Mozambique 1993-2009."

2   Jenkins, *Urbanization, Urbanism and Urbanity.*

3   Jenkins, "Home Space: Context Report."

4   Paulo et al, "Xiculongo: Social Relations of Urban Poverty in Maputo."

5   Raimundo et al, "The State of Food Insecurity in Maputo, Mozambique."

6   War on Want, *Forces for Change: Informal Economy Organisations in Africa.*

7   Kamete and Lindell, "The Politics of 'Non-Planning' Interventions in African Cities."

8   Ulset, "Formalization of Informal Marketplaces."

9   Dibben et al, "Towards and Against Formalization."

10  Raimundo, *Gender, Choice and Migration.*

11  Interview with President of Mukhero Cross Border Trade Association, Maputo, 3 September 2014.

12  de Vletter and Polana, "Female Itinerant Maize Traders in Southern Mozambique"; Peberdy, "Border Crossings"; Peberdy and Rogerson, "Transnationalism and Non-South African Entrepreneurs"; Peberdy et al, "Transnational Entrepreneurship and Informal Cross Border Trade with South Africa."

13  Macamo, "Estimates of Unrecorded Cross-Border Trade."

14  Peberdy et al, "Transnational Entrepreneurship and Informal Cross Border Trade."

15  Peberdy, "Border Crossings"

16  Peberdy, "Mobile Entrepreneurship."

17  Peberdy and Rogerson, "Transnationalism and Non-South African Entrepreneurs."

18  Peberdy, "Border Crossings"

19  Peberdy et al, "Transnational Entrepreneurship and Informal Cross Border Trade."

20  Peberdy and Crush, "Invisible Trade, Invisible Travellers."

21  Söderbaum, "Blocking Human Potential."

22  War on Want, *Forces for Change: Informal Economy Organisations in Africa.*

23  Ibid.

24  Dibben et al, "Towards and Against Formalization."

25  War on Want, *Forces for Change: Informal Economy Organisations in Africa.*

26  de Oliveira et al, "Developments and Competitiveness of Mozambican Chicken Meat Industry."

27  Brooks, "Riches from Rags or Persistent Poverty?"

28  Brooks, *Clothing Poverty.*

29  de Vletter and Polana, "Female Itinerant Maize Traders in Southern Mozambique"; Peberdy, "Border Crossings"; Peberdy et al., "Transnational Entrepreneurship and Informal Cross Border Trade with South Africa."

30  Raimundo, *Gender, Choice and Migration.*

31  Macamo, "Estimates of Unrecorded Cross-Border Trade."

32  Raimundo, *Gender, Choice and Migration.*

33  Raimundo et al. "The State of Food Insecurity in Maputo."

34  Tawodzera et al, "International Migrants and Refugees in Cape Town's Informal Economy."

35  Finmark Trust, "FinScope Mozambique Survey, 2009: Survey Report."

36  Baxter and Allwright, "Opportunities to Improve Financial Inclusion in Mozambique"; War on Want, *Forces for Change: Informal Economy Organisations in Africa*; Interview with Armindo Chembane, Executive Secretary of ASSOTSI, May 2015.

37  Baxter and Allwright, "Opportunities to Improve Financial Inclusion in Mozambique."

38  Interview with Program Officer of Business Growth Scheme Manager (PACDE – Enterprise

Competitiveness and Private Sector Development Project), Maputo, 25 November 2014.

39  Becker, *The Informal Economy*; ILO, "Child Labour and the Urban Informal Sector in Uganda."

40  Burra, "Crusading for Children in India's Informal Economy."

41  Peberdy et al, "Transnational Entrepreneurship and Informal Cross Border Trade."

42  Crush and Ramachandran, "Doing Business with Xenophobia."

43  The Common Customs Tariff is composed of 97 categories of products and sub products.

44  Chair of Mukhero Association, Maputo, 03/09/2014.

45  Ibid.

46  Focus Group Discussion, Zimpeto market, 05/12/2014.

47  Crush and Ramachandran, "Doing Business with Xenophobia."

## REFERENCES

1.  M. Baxter, and L. Allwright, "Opportunities to Improve Financial Inclusion in Mozambique: Building on Investments and Economic Activities Associated with the Extractives Sector" Report by OzMozis for FSDMoç (Financial Sector Deepening – Mozambique), 2015.

2.  K.F. Becker, *The Informal Economy: Fact Finding Study* (Stockholm: SIDA, 2004).

3.  A. Brooks, "Riches from Rags or Persistent Poverty? The Working Lives of Secondhand Clothing Vendors in Maputo, Mozambique. *Textile: The Journal of Cloth & Culture*, 10(2012): 222-237.

4.  A. Brooks, *Clothing Poverty: The Hidden World of Fast Fashion and Second-Hand Clothes* (London: Zed Books, 2015).

5.  N. Burra, "Crusading for Children in India's Informal Economy" *Economic and Political Weekly* 40(2005): 5199-5208.

6.  J. Crush and S. Ramachandran, "Doing Business with Xenophobia" In J. Crush, A. Chikanda and C. Skinner (eds.) *Mean Streets: Migration, Xenophobia and Informality in South Africa* (Cape Town: SAMP, ACC, IDRC, 2015), pp. 25-59.

7.  P. Dibben, G. Wood and C. Williams, "Towards and Against Formalization: Regulation and Change in Informal Work in Mozambique" *International Labour Review* 154(2015): 373-392.

8.  C. de Oliveira, D. Pivoto, C. Spanhol and V. Corte, "Developments and Competitiveness of Mozambican Chicken Meat Industry" *RAIMED – Revista de Administração IMED*, 5(2015): 205-216.

9.  F. de Vletter, and E. Polana, "Female Itinerant Maize Traders in Southern Mozambique: A Study of a Higher-End Informal Sector Activity and its Potential for Poverty Reduction." ILO/SAMAT Discussion Paper No. 17, International Labour Organization, Geneva, 2001.

10. Finmark Trust, "FinScope Mozambique Survey, 2009: Survey Report" Finmark Trust, Johannesburg, December, 2009.

11. ILO, "Child Labour and the Urban Informal Sector in Uganda" ILO and Government of Uganda, Kampala, 2004.

12. P. Jenkins, "Home Space: Context Report" Danish Research Council, Copenhagen, 2012.

13. P. Jenkins, *Urbanization, Urbanism and Urbanity: Home Spaces and House Cultures in an African City* (New York: Palgrave Macmillan, 2013).

14. S. Jones and F. Tarp, "Jobs and Welfare in Mozambique" WIDER Working Paper No. 2013/045, United Nations University – World Institute for Development Economics Research (UNU-WIDER), 2013.

15. A. Kamete and I. Lindell, "The Politics of "Non-Planning" Interventions in African Cities: Unravelling the International and Local Dimensions in Harare and Maputo" *Journal of Southern African Studies*, 36(2010): 889-912.

16. J. Macamo, "Estimates of Unrecorded Cross-Border Trade between Mozambique and her Neighbors: Implications for Food Security" Technical Paper No. 88, U.S. Agency for International Development (USAID), Washington, DC, 1999.

17. A. Nucifora and L. da Silva, "Rapid Growth and Economic Transformation in Mozambique 1993-2009". In P. Chuhan-Pole and M. Angwafo (eds.) *Yes, Africa Can: Success Stories from a Dynamic Continent* (Washington, DC: World Bank, 2011), pp. 65-80.

18. M. Paulo, C. Rosário and I. Tvedten, "Xiculongo: Social Relations of Urban Poverty in Maputo, Mozambique" Report No 13, Chr. Michelsen Institute, Bergen, Norway, 2007.

19. S. Peberdy and C. Rogerson, "Transnationalism and Non-South African Entrepreneurs in South Africa's Small, Medium and Micro-Enterprise (SMME) Economy" *Canadian Journal of African Studies*, 34(2000): 20-40.

20. S. Peberdy and J. Crush, "Invisible Trade, Invisible Travellers: The Maputo Corridor Spatial Development Initiative and Informal Cross Border Trading" *South African Geographical Journal*, 83(2001): 115-123.

21. S. Peberdy, "Border Crossings: Small Entrepreneurs and Informal Sector Cross Border Trade between South Africa and Mozambique" *Tjidschrift voor Economische en Sociale Geographie*, 91(2000): 361-378.

22. S. Peberdy, "Mobile Entrepreneurship: Informal Sector Cross-Border Trade and Street Trade in South Africa" *Development Southern Africa*, 17(2000): 201-219.

23. S. Peberdy, J. Crush, D. Tevera, E. Campbell, N. Zindela, I. Raimundo, T. Green, A. Chikanda and G. Tawodzera, "Transnational Entrepreneurship and Informal Cross Border Trade with South Africa" In J. Crush, A. Chikanda and C. Skinner (eds.) *Mean Streets: Migration, Xenophobia and Informality in South Africa* (Cape Town: SAMP, ACC, IDRC, 2015), pp. 207-228.

24. I. Raimundo, *Gender, Choice and Migration: Household Dynamics and Urbanisation in Mozambique* (Saarbrucken, Germany: Verlag Dr. Muller Aktiengesellschaft & Co. KG, 2010).

25. I. Raimundo, J. Crush and W. Pendleton, *The State of Food Insecurity in Maputo, Mozambique* AFSUN Urban Food Security Series No. 20, Cape Town, 2014.

26. F. Söderbaum, "Blocking Human Potential: How Formal Policies Block the Informal Economy in the Maputo Corridor." In B. Guha-Khasnobis, R. Kanbur and E. Ostrom, (eds.) *Linking the Formal and Informal Economy: Concepts and Policies* (Oxford: Oxford University Press, 2007), pp.163–179.

27. G. Tawodzera, A. Chikanda, J. Crush and R. Tengeh, *International Migrants and Refugees in Cape Town's Informal Economy* SAMP Migration Policy Series No. 70, Southern African Migration Programme, Cape Town, 2015.

28. D. Thorsen, "Children Working in the Urban Informal Economy: Evidence from West and Central Africa" UNICEF, Dakar, 2012.

29. A. Ulset, "Formalization of Informal Marketplaces: A Case Study of the Xikhelene Market, Maputo, Mozambique" M.A. Thesis, University of Oslo, 2010.

30. War on Want, *Forces for Change: Informal Economy Organisations in Africa* (London: War on Want, 2006).

## MIGRATION POLICY SERIES

1 *Covert Operations: Clandestine Migration, Temporary Work and Immigration Policy in South Africa* (1997) ISBN 1-874864-51-9

2 *Riding the Tiger: Lesotho Miners and Permanent Residence in South Africa* (1997) ISBN 1-874864-52-7

3 *International Migration, Immigrant Entrepreneurs and South Africa's Small Enterprise Economy* (1997) ISBN 1-874864-62-4

4 *Silenced by Nation Building: African Immigrants and Language Policy in the New South Africa* (1998) ISBN 1-874864-64-0

5 *Left Out in the Cold? Housing and Immigration in the New South Africa* (1998) ISBN 1-874864-68-3

6 *Trading Places: Cross-Border Traders and the South African Informal Sector* (1998) ISBN 1-874864-71-3

7 *Challenging Xenophobia: Myth and Realities about Cross-Border Migration in Southern Africa* (1998) ISBN 1-874864-70-5

8 *Sons of Mozambique: Mozambican Miners and Post-Apartheid South Africa* (1998) ISBN 1-874864-78-0

9 *Women on the Move: Gender and Cross-Border Migration to South Africa* (1998) ISBN 1-874864-82-9.

10 *Namibians on South Africa: Attitudes Towards Cross-Border Migration and Immigration Policy* (1998) ISBN 1-874864-84-5.

11 *Building Skills: Cross-Border Migrants and the South African Construction Industry* (1999) ISBN 1-874864-84-5

12 *Immigration & Education: International Students at South African Universities and Technikons* (1999) ISBN 1-874864-89-6

13 *The Lives and Times of African Immigrants in Post-Apartheid South Africa* (1999) ISBN 1-874864-91-8

14 *Still Waiting for the Barbarians: South African Attitudes to Immigrants and Immigration* (1999) ISBN 1-874864-91-8

15 *Undermining Labour: Migrancy and Sub-Contracting in the South African Gold Mining Industry* (1999) ISBN 1-874864-91-8

16 *Borderline Farming: Foreign Migrants in South African Commercial Agriculture* (2000) ISBN 1-874864-97-7

17 *Writing Xenophobia: Immigration and the Press in Post-Apartheid South Africa* (2000) ISBN 1-919798-01-3

18 *Losing Our Minds: Skills Migration and the South African Brain Drain* (2000) ISBN 1-919798-03-x

19 *Botswana: Migration Perspectives and Prospects* (2000) ISBN 1-919798-04-8

20 *The Brain Gain: Skilled Migrants and Immigration Policy in Post-Apartheid South Africa* (2000) ISBN 1-919798-14-5

21 *Cross-Border Raiding and Community Conflict in the Lesotho-South African Border Zone* (2001) ISBN 1-919798-16-1

22 *Immigration, Xenophobia and Human Rights in South Africa* (2001) ISBN 1-919798-30-7

23 *Gender and the Brain Drain from South Africa* (2001) ISBN 1-919798-35-8

24 *Spaces of Vulnerability: Migration and HIV/AIDS in South Africa* (2002) ISBN 1-919798-38-2

25 *Zimbabweans Who Move: Perspectives on International Migration in Zimbabwe* (2002) ISBN 1-919798-40-4

26 *The Border Within: The Future of the Lesotho-South African International Boundary* (2002) ISBN 1-919798-41-2

27 *Mobile Namibia: Migration Trends and Attitudes* (2002) ISBN 1-919798-44-7

28 *Changing Attitudes to Immigration and Refugee Policy in Botswana* (2003) ISBN 1-919798-47-1

29 *The New Brain Drain from Zimbabwe* (2003) ISBN 1-919798-48-X

30 *Regionalizing Xenophobia? Citizen Attitudes to Immigration and Refugee Policy in Southern Africa* (2004) ISBN 1-919798-53-6

31 *Migration, Sexuality and HIV/AIDS in Rural South Africa* (2004) ISBN 1-919798-63-3

32 *Swaziland Moves: Perceptions and Patterns of Modern Migration* (2004) ISBN 1-919798-67-6

33 *HIV/AIDS and Children's Migration in Southern Africa* (2004) ISBN 1-919798-70-6

34 *Medical Leave: The Exodus of Health Professionals from Zimbabwe* (2005) ISBN 1-919798-74-9

35 *Degrees of Uncertainty: Students and the Brain Drain in Southern Africa* (2005) ISBN 1-919798-84-6

36 *Restless Minds: South African Students and the Brain Drain* (2005) ISBN 1-919798-82-X

37 *Understanding Press Coverage of Cross-Border Migration in Southern Africa since 2000* (2005) ISBN 1-919798-91-9

38 *Northern Gateway: Cross-Border Migration Between Namibia and Angola* (2005) ISBN 1-919798-92-7

39 *Early Departures: The Emigration Potential of Zimbabwean Students* (2005) ISBN 1-919798-99-4

40 *Migration and Domestic Workers: Worlds of Work, Health and Mobility in Johannesburg* (2005) ISBN 1-920118-02-0

41 *The Quality of Migration Services Delivery in South Africa* (2005) ISBN 1-920118-03-9

42 *States of Vulnerability: The Future Brain Drain of Talent to South Africa* (2006) ISBN 1-920118-07-1

43 *Migration and Development in Mozambique: Poverty, Inequality and Survival* (2006) ISBN 1-920118-10-1

44 *Migration, Remittances and Development in Southern Africa* (2006) ISBN 1-920118-15-2

45 *Medical Recruiting: The Case of South African Health Care Professionals* (2007) ISBN 1-920118-47-0

46 *Voices From the Margins: Migrant Women's Experiences in Southern Africa* (2007) ISBN 1-920118-50-0

47 *The Haemorrhage of Health Professionals From South Africa: Medical Opinions* (2007) ISBN 978-1-920118-63-1

48 *The Quality of Immigration and Citizenship Services in Namibia* (2008) ISBN 978-1-920118-67-9

49 *Gender, Migration and Remittances in Southern Africa* (2008) ISBN 978-1-920118-70-9

50 *The Perfect Storm: The Realities of Xenophobia in Contemporary South Africa* (2008) ISBN 978-1-920118-71-6

51 *Migrant Remittances and Household Survival in Zimbabwe* (2009) ISBN 978-1-920118-92-1

52 *Migration, Remittances and 'Development' in Lesotho* (2010) ISBN 978-1-920409-26-5

53 *Migration-Induced HIV and AIDS in Rural Mozambique and Swaziland* (2011) ISBN 978-1-920409-49-4

54 *Medical Xenophobia: Zimbabwean Access to Health Services in South Africa* (2011) ISBN 978-1-920409-63-0

55 *The Engagement of the Zimbabwean Medical Diaspora* (2011) ISBN 978-1-920409-64-7

56 *Right to the Classroom: Educational Barriers for Zimbabweans in South Africa* (2011) ISBN 978-1-920409-68-5

57 *Patients Without Borders: Medical Tourism and Medical Migration in Southern Africa* (2012) ISBN 978-1-920409-74-6

58 *The Disengagement of the South African Medical Diaspora* (2012) ISBN 978-1-920596-00-2

59 *The Third Wave: Mixed Migration from Zimbabwe to South Africa* (2012) ISBN 978-1-920596-01-9

60 *Linking Migration, Food Security and Development* (2012) ISBN 978-1-920596-02-6

61 *Unfriendly Neighbours: Contemporary Migration from Zimbabwe to Botswana* (2012) ISBN 978-1-920596-16-3

62 *Heading North: The Zimbabwean Diaspora in Canada* (2012) ISBN 978-1-920596-03-3

63 *Dystopia and Disengagement: Diaspora Attitudes Towards South Africa* (2012) ISBN 978-1-920596-04-0

64 *Soft Targets: Xenophobia, Public Violence and Changing Attitudes to Migrants in South Africa after May 2008* (2013) ISBN 978-1-920596-05-7

65 *Brain Drain and Regain: Migration Behaviour of South African Medical Professionals* (2014) ISBN 978-1-920596-07-1

66 *Xenophobic Violence in South Africa: Denialism, Minimalism, Realism* (2014) ISBN 978-1-920596-08-8

67 *Migrant Entrepreneurship Collective Violence and Xenophobia in South Africa* (2014) ISBN 978-1-920596-09-5

68 *Informal Migrant Entrepreneurship and Inclusive Growth in South Africa, Zimbabwe and Mozambique* (2015) ISBN 978-1-920596-10-1

69 *Calibrating Informal Cross-Border Trade in Southern Africa* (2015) ISBN 978-1-920596-13-2

70 *International Migrants and Refugees in Cape Town's Informal Economy* (2016) ISBN 978-1-920596-15-6

71 *International Migrants in Johannesburg's Informal Economy* (2016) ISBN 978-1-920596-18-7

72 *Food Remittances: Migration and Food Security in Africa* (2016) ISBN 978-1-920596-19-4